Feed Your Piggy Bank!

Practical and Easy-To-Do Money-Saving Tips

By: Deborah Evans

9781635012835

I0510831

PUBLISHERS NOTES

Disclaimer – Speedy Publishing LLC

Speedy Publishing LLC

40 E Main Street, Newark, Delaware, 19711

Contact Us: 1-888-248-4521

Website: http://www.speedypublishing.co

REPRINTED Paperback Edition: 9781635012835:

Manufactured in the United States of America

DEDICATION

This book is dedicated to Mom. When I was younger, you taught me the true value of money. Thank you. Today, I teach the same lesson to the younger generation. .

TABLE OF CONTENTS

Chapter 1 - How to Create a Comfortable Savings Plan

Ideally a young working adult should be able to comfortably save about 10% of his or her income. The individual should then be disciplined enough to save this amount without touching or tapping into it for unnecessary and frivolous expenditure. If this is successfully achieved then the individual would be able to venture into other types of commitments on a long term basis without the probability of defaulting at the first sign of a challenge or trouble.

Curbing lifestyles and keeping within a planned budget will also allow the individual to comfortable create a savings plan that will be useful in times of need.

These needs can be when a job is lost, when medical emergencies arise, when a good deal comes along, when opportunity strikes and any other positive venture that might require instant access to considerable funds.

Feed Your Piggy Bank!

Thus learning to develop the savings attitude will eventually prove to be beneficial both in the present and for future opportunities.

Drawing up a savings plan that can be put into practice over a yearly time frame would eventually help the individual create a very healthy savings amount.

This would then allow the individual to focus better on the needs rather than the wants of the daily requirements of existence. It would also allow the individual to learn how to spend less in order to save more.

There are several tools available to assist an individual in creating and tracking a complete savings plan. These can be monitored periodically depending on the individual's preferences.

How Much Are You Spending Daily?

People are amazed to see how much they spend per week when they add up their day to day spending. If you're like most people, you enjoy that trip to the coffee shop every morning or lunch out with friends. Instead of that $4 latte at Starbucks, try brewing coffee at home and bringing it to work in a travel mug. You'll save tons of money this way and have an entire pot of coffee for about one third of the cost of one cup, maybe even less! Skip the fast food lunches and bring in a sandwich, some chips, and a cup of yogurt to work for lunch. Not only will you eat healthier, you will find that you're saving about fifty dollars per week in lunches!

For many people, it's the splurges in life that can break the bank. Going out to the bar with friends or having a steak dinner can be fun, but it can also be quite expensive. Instead, invite friends over and have some food on the grill. Get everyone to bring in their own beer and other beverages. You will have just as much fun with close friends without spending a pretty penny on a dinner check, bar, tab, and tips.

The movies can be a good time, too, but they can also be a bit expensive, especially when you add in drinks and popcorn. Today's technology allows you to watch new releases on demand or over the Internet for much less than a theater ticket. An added bonus: you can pause and use the restroom without missing a thing!

Groceries can add up fast, especially for people with children. There are lots of ways you can cut spending in this aspect of daily life. Clip coupons and look for buy one get one free or half off sales at your local grocery store or mass merchandiser. Coupons are literally like having cash in hand, so it makes sense to use them as often as possible. Make grocery lists and only buy the things you need for that particular week. Wholesale clubs can be a real money saver for families who need to buy large quantities of items in bulk. Things like paper towels, shampoo, and peanut butter can all be bought in larger quantities at a discounted price. Dollar stores are also a great place to buy things like cleaning supplies, toothbrushes, and other small household items without paying full price.

Even with mass transportation such as subways and the city bus, most people still opt to commute to work using their cars. While this is convenient, it can also be costly. In addition, owning a car is an expensive venture. If you live near some coworkers, consider doing a carpool.

Carpools are a good way to save on gas and on wear and tear to your car. Plus, it's an excellent way to get to know your fellow coworkers. If you drive to and from work, make sure your tires are properly inflated at the factory recommended PSI. Studies have shown that underinflated tires can waste gas, and causes extra wear on your tires. By ensuring that your tires are inflated properly, you can save on gas usage and on the tires themselves.

While getting an oil change can sometimes be time consuming, it is absolutely imperative to the longevity of your car. Make sure you get your oil changed every few thousand miles. Most local garages offer oil change specials and have coupons in the local newspaper. National chains also usually offer oil change discounts through printable coupons online.

Properly maintaining your car can save you thousands of dollars in repairs and extend the overall life of your car. Another secret many people might not be aware of is that some national auto parts stores will change your car battery for no charge if you buy the battery at their store.

Premium gas costs more, but really offers little benefits to your car. If you use regular unleaded, you're probably paying several cents less per gallon, and getting the same results. Another important rule of thumb for car owners is to avoid taking your vehicle back to the dealer for repairs. Dealerships have been known to charge much more for the same work, and often tend to "find" more wrong with your car. Instead, take your car to a small, independent shop with a good reputation. Ask friends for some advice or recommendations on a good mechanic. You can replace simple things like headlights, wiper blades, and air filters yourself for a fraction of the cost. Also, be sure to change out your antifreeze each winter.

CHAPTER 2- WHAT MAKES SAVING MONEY SO IMPORTANT?

Learning to save as much as possible is always a good habit to form, thus there is no real need to have a reason to practice this positive attitudes than for its sheer benefits which are rather extensive.

However if there needs to be a reason to save more the following are just some of the more prominent ones to go by:

• Having a healthy emergency fund that is accumulated through diligent savings, is always beneficial. This will help the individual tap into this resource when the need arises, as compared to having to resort to taking out a loan which will only incur high interest rates, that may cause the budgeting process of the individual to be severely affected.

- Creating a good long term saving plan will also allow the individual the option of making huge down payments thus eliminating the need for larger loan packages and financing help. With more savings the individual is able to bargain better as the saving will allow for cash payments to be made. This will present quite an advantage to the individual when the seller is keep to transact quickly.

- Saving more will also allow the individual to have the resources available to cash in on bargains and sudden opportunities whenever and wherever they pop up. Often people allow opportunities to pass them by simply because they lack the finances to capitalize on them. Therefore learning to save more and frequently putting aside any assess cash will keep the individual from missing out when it most counts.

- Making the effort to save more will also inculcate in the individual the opportunity to be very disciplined and focused, which is a trait that will help in other areas in his or her life too. The sooner this trait is cultivated in an individual the sooner it will bear positive results.

Cutting Family Spending without Sacrificing Welfare

There comes a time in every family where we have to evaluate our spending and start looking out for the future. Times are tough and if we're not careful, we'll go through our savings only to end up back at square one.

Perhaps you haven't yet been able to save and you feel as if developing a family budget is far too difficult. Well, as a working mother of five, I'm here to tell you that despite your expenses and the size of your family there are still ways to effectively budget, save money and make every dollar stretch further than ever before.

If you're struggling to make ends meet at the end of every month, or you are falling into ever-growing debt, now is the time to rework your finances so that you can improve your lifestyle and protect your family's future. Regardless of your income, there are ways to cut corners and save money.

Keep in mind that developing a family budget doesn't mean that you can't occasionally splurge or that you need to restrict your family in any way. In fact, it's quite the opposite.

Your mindset will be to curb spending where it's not directly benefiting your family in the long run, and to stretch, invest and make better purchase decisions. In other words, it's about making your money go further - and work harder for you and your family.

Creating a budget will also help you identify "cash leaks" quickly, and in many cases, you may not even notice where a good portion of your money is going.

We all make "routine" purchases and just based on our lifestyle choices and habits alone, we can end up spending twice as much as we really have to. For example, do you visit the grocery store more than three times a week to purchase meals and supplies for your family? If so, cutting this down to one trip a week and getting everything you need at once will instantly reduce your spending. Not only will you purchase only what you need, but you'll be able to design your shopping around current weekly specials, so that you are taking advantage of coupons and discounts.

Feed Your Piggy Bank!

Your budget can be as flexible as you're comfortable with as well, changing as you make more money, or as your family requires. This report was written to provide you with the ability to create a systematic process where you can easily start saving more money each month, and improving your family's lifestyle while protecting your future.

CHAPTER 3- EVALUATE HOW YOU'RE SPENDING YOUR MONEY

For most of us, we're living on a fixed income where we know what to expect with each paycheck each month, and if that's the case with you, you'll find it much easier to strategically develop a budget plan for your family.

If you are an entrepreneur or working in a job where your income fluctuates, you can still develop a budget but you'll need to make sure it accommodates any possible decrease in income each month.

The first step in developing a budget is to take stock of your fiscal situation. Assess exactly where you are in your financial life, taking inventory of all expenses on a month-to-month basis.

When you begin to list the different expenses you have, you'll gain a better idea as to how you need to better manage your money, while identifying potential ways of saving a bit of money each month. Remember, you don't have to save hundreds a month, but instead, work within a budget that helps you pay the bills, while putting a little aside every month. It will add up quickly.

When evaluating your expenses and spending, you need to begin by writing down your bills but make sure you also analyze bank statements and credit card accounts. You want to keep an eye out on "casual spending" where you are spending money on places that aren't really necessary.

Budgeting begins with self-evaluating your own spending, and then taking a closer look at your monthly bills to determine whether there are ways of consolidating your expenses to make it more manageable for your family.

When going through your expenses and identifying key areas where you can save money, be sure to include a detailed list that segments your spending into categories. For example, your spreadsheet could include "Obligatory Spending" such as your mortgage or rent payment, as well as "Necessities" which include food and utilities.

Then, include "Pocket Expenses" including entertainment and of course, "Family Allowances" that may include family trips, clothing, home improvements, and misc. events and items. The more you create a detailed overview of your spending and overall costs, the easier it will be to identify areas where you can cut spending and save more money.

Writing your expenditures down often sheds a lot of light on areas in your financial life that could be 'tweaked', and that extra bit of money each month will go a long way.

A budget helps your entire family focus on common goals. It is unifying families in mutual purpose and effort, working together towards a successful outcome and reward. In addition, setting a family budget helps you prepare for emergencies as well as unexpected expenses.

Tip: One of the easiest ways to get the kids involved is by offering them a weekly allowance in exchange for doing odd jobs around the house, or set up a bank account for each of your children and deposits their earnings on a regular basis, showing them statements of their account growing over time. Not only will this help them learn how to budget, but also teach them a very valuable lesson about responsibility.

Do You Need a Financial Workout?

Keeping track of one's personal financial statues is something that can be practiced or learnt with some tips and careful and diligent observations. In order to have healthy financial standing the individual should take a serious view on cultivating good and wise spending habits very early on.

The following are some areas which some focused attention can benefit from when it comes to keeping finances in shape:

• Being a weary and informed buyer is a good attitude to cultivate, as this will be pivotal in ensuring the individual does not easily get carried away or taken in by savvy sales personal making impressive sales pitches. Know the attributes of any item intended to be bought, before actually making the physical purchase, will ensure complete satisfaction from a product that not only suits the needs but is also considered essential. Failing to ensure these two important points before making a purchase would deem the purchase frivolous thus a waste of money.

Feed Your Piggy Bank!

- Buying on credit is a habit that should either be broken or controlled to its maximum, as this form of making purchases does not allow the individual to be completely conscious of just how much is being spent. Learning to make as many purchases as possible using cash has a better shock and controlling element that using credit. There is nothing more effective and eye opening for the individual, then to see his or her cash depleting at an alarming rate, which is evident through cash transactions.

- Although the means for making purchases may be available for the individual, being able to discern what is necessary and what is not is also a form of keeping finances in shape. When there is an excess amount of money available, there is always the tendency to want to make use of it, and most times it is used for the wrong purposes. One way of avoiding this, is to find savings plans that don't encourage easy withdrawals.

Define Your Priorities then a Successful Strategy

In order to develop a successful strategy that helps you save money every month, you need to begin by defining your priorities. Begin by writing down the most important aspects of your life, as well as what you want for your family. Priorities are similar to goals except rather than defining milestones, you simply create an overview of what you are hoping to achieve.

Once you have listed your family priorities, you then determine your goals. With goals, you are defining a specific amount of money that you'd like to save within a certain time frame. Setting goals is incredibly important, because it keeps you on track while giving you the opportunity to see your progress every step of the way.

Make sure your goals are reasonable ones! You want to set yourself up for success, not failure and so it's important to truly evaluate your income and come up with a reasonable amount you can save each month. Your goals could also include making future purchases or payments. For example, your goal could be to save 10% of your monthly income for a child's college fund.

Limit your goals to 2-3 per priority. You want to maintain focus and be able to stay on track without feeling overwhelmed. Once you have determined your priorities and goals, it's time to work towards reaching them! Your entire family will need to get involved in this, so it's time to have a family meeting where you discuss the benefits of setting goals and budgeting as a family, highlighting the rewards so that your family is focused on the same goals that you are.

Track your progress, communicate with your family every step of the way, and maintain a system that allows you to quickly monitor your progress (and success!) Make it easy for your family to save more money by always being on the lookout for ways of reducing your spending without sacrificing the most important things in your life.

Consider the frequency in which your family eats out, examine your commute for more efficient driving, pay larger bills in portions throughout the month, rather than all at once, and shop based on weekly specials. Once you get into the habit of making more conscious decisions about your spending, you'll find it easier to save more money than ever before.

If You Promise to Make Financial Amendments, Act On Them

Making resolutions is easy but making them stick is something else which requires much more than just some words and thoughts. In the quest to make financial resolutions that eventually see some level of success there needs to be some careful planning and thought exercised beforehand.

The following are some tips to help an individual design and stick to a set of financial resolutions effectively and successfully:

• Perhaps the oldest and most common recommendation would be to physically note down the goal intended to be reached, through the financial resolution exercise. These goals should be designed to follow a very real and practical format that will create the encouragement for the individual to follow it well. Seeing something is writing is somehow more effective especially if the written goal is placed in a very visible and frequented area.

• Besides writing and visualizing these resolutions there should also be short term incentives included in the whole exercise to keep the individual motivated to stick to the financial resolutions made. Such rewards may include an occasional treat or a small present to note the significance of the effort extended towards keeping the financial resolution. Celebrating such efforts periodically will ensure the individual does keeps steadfast in the quest to focus on keeping the resolution, and yet at the same time it will help to avoid making the individual feel deprived in any way.

• Thinking of the goals frequently is also another practice that should be encouraged as it will help to fuel the resolution keeping mindset to continue being steadfast and disciplined. It will keep the idea of giving up at bay and any negative challenges from becoming overwhelming. This "fuel" is usually the important factor that keeps the resolution very much alive and achievable. Dedicate some quiet time each day to focus on the resolution and tap into the inner strength available.

CHAPTER 4- CUTTING DOWN ON EXPENSES FOR ADDED SAVINGS

1. Harness the sun's energy through solar powered light fixtures. There are lots of light fixtures today that can be powered by the sunlight. In using them, you would be able to save lots of money, since your electricity bills would go down. All you have to do is to shop for these items at your local store, or even through the web. Some of these items are even very easy to install and are available in DIY kits.

2. Use your car sparingly.

* Walk towards the grocery store. The price of gasoline these days continue to go up, which is why it is a good idea to come up with ways to lessen your vehicle usage. One of which would be to walk towards the grocery store, especially if it is just a few blocks away

from your place. Make it fun by walking with your spouse, so that aside from saving money, you both can also shed some weight.

* Ride the bus instead of using your car. If you are going somewhere, which is not possible to reach by merely walking, then you should ride the bus, instead of using the car. Riding a bus or a train can only cost you a few dollars, compared to filling up your car with lots of gasoline. Just prepare earlier, and take note of the schedule of the bus, so that you won't be late.

3. Save on electricity.

* Open your windows instead of turning on the fan. When it is hot, you may want to turn on the fan or even your air conditioning system, in order to improve the temperature at your place. To save money, instead of using them, you can always open up your windows. By doing that, you can benefit from fresh air, aside from saving money. To make it cooler, you can always put some ice in front of the fan if you want to.

* Also, turn off your computer when not in use. There are lots of people today who turn on their computers at the beginning of the day, and only turn it off before sleeping at nights. If you are one of them, then you should turn it off, prior to stepping outside your place. By doing that, you can ensure that you would be consuming lesser amounts of energy. Aside from that, it can also prolong the life of your computer.

* Turn off the television. Becoming addicted to the television is one of the things that can cause your electricity bills to soar higher. Thus, you need to turn it off, when you are not watching. Aside from that, you should also minimize the times that you try to watch TV, when you are actually doing another thing

* Turn off the lights at your place when you leave. You may feel more secure in leaving your place while the lights are turned on. However, it can be one of the factors that affect your energy bills. Thus, you should turn the lights off when you leave. If you want, you can still leave just a single light on, so that you would feel secure when you go out.

* Turn off your electric stove earlier. Whenever you are using your electric stove to cook a meal, you should make it a practice to turn it off earlier than usual. This is because the plate on your stove usually stays heated even when the power is turned off. Thus, if you turn it off a few minutes early, then it can still continue to provide heat to your recipe.

* Don't leave the door of the refrigerator open. Leaving the door of your refrigerator open for a long period of time can cost you lot of money, due to using up lots of energy. This is because whenever you open your refrigerator, it could lose a certain amount of its cool temperature, and will have to try to attain it again. Thus, tell all the members of your family about this, so that you can minimize your energy consumption.

5. It's fun to wash your own car. The cost of having your car washed through a car washing station on a weekly basis can easily pile up over the months. Thus, if you are going to wash your own car, then you would be able to save lots of money. Aside from that, it can also provide you the exercise that you need, in order to stay as fit as you can be.

6. Watch what you eat.

* Be healthy. The cost of medicines today continues to go up, especially when it comes to antibiotics. To ensure that you won't have to reach for your pocket to buy them, you need to maintain

your health. To achieve that, you should get enough exercise on a regular basis. Aside from that, you should also take a multivitamin supplement in conjunction with a healthy diet.

* Try to enjoy leftovers. When you eat at restaurants, cook up some delicious meals for a family gathering or prepare for a birthday party, you can be sure that you would have a bunch of leftovers inside your refrigerator after. Heating them up for your meals instead of throwing them away could save you a lot of money.

* Eat lesser amounts of meat. When you compare meat products to vegetables, they are more expensive, aside from the fact that they are often associated with fats. Thus, it is best to eat more vegetables instead. However, since you need meat for your source of protein, you should opt for chicken without its skin, since they are more affordable.

* Cook your own meals. Cooking your own meals could help you save lots of money. This is because buying the ingredients for a certain recipe is definitively more affordable, than eating out in restaurants or fast food chains. Just make sure to cook healthy meals, so that you can also ensure that you are getting the nutrients you need.

* Eat in a slower pace. When it comes to eating, you can save more money and lose weight by eating slower. This is because when you eat slowly, you will have a tendency to eat less, since your stomach would take a certain time to send a message to your brain that it is already full. Thus, in eating slower, you won't just enjoy a fitter you, but you can also enjoy more savings since you consume lesser amounts of foods

* Bring your own lunch. If you don't have the time to go home and eat lunch, you should cook your own food and bring it with you. By doing this, you won't have to spend lots of money in eating at restaurants or fast food chains. Aside from saving lots of money, you can also ensure that you stay in good health, since you would be the one to prepare it.

* Eat healthier meals. Avoiding highly processed foods is actually something that offers more than just health benefits. It can also help you save up some money, since they usually cost more than when you prepare your own meals. Preparing your own meals can help you save money, since you can easily load it up vegetables, which are more affordable than meat.

7. Save on water. Don't turn on the water faucet at its maximum level. When you take a bath, there is no need to turn on the water at its maximum level, especially if you are not in a rush. Turning it at higher levels can make your water bills soar high. Thus, if you take control of it, then you should be able to save some money by conserving water more effectively.

8. Impose a dollar limit when buying.

* Buy basic things in wholesale prices. There are lots of basic things that a person needs, and buying it in retail prices can pile up the cost. Thus, it is best if you buy them in bulk, since that would give you a chance to purchase them in wholesale prices. In doing this, you would be able to save lots of money, aside from the fact that you can have good supply of your needs.

* Buy used items. Buying used items compared to buying those that are brand new is definitely more affordable. Thus, if you want to save money, then you should begin shopping around for used

products. To find them, you can always go through the internet, visit garage sales, or check out some local auctions.

* Buy an alternative. When you do your research, you would find out many of the products you need have cheaper substitutes. Thus, you should consider purchasing the substitutes of the items that you need, which are more affordable, but can offer you the same thing. For example, instead of buying a high end branded item, you can check out its equally competitive alternative, which can offer the same features at a lower price.

* Look for coupons. There are lots of coupons available today, which you can access through the internet. These coupons can offer you discounts on certain fast food chains, restaurants, as well as in local stores. All you have to do is to sign up for the websites that offer them, and follow the simple instructions provided.

* Take advantage of sale, especially after the holidays. Taking advantage of sale, especially those that are offered after the holidays can help you save lots of cash. For example, in most cases, decorations would become very affordable after the Christmas season. Thus, if you want to save money, you can always purchase them for the following year.

* You can always say no. If your kids are quite fond of telling you what they want at the grocery store or at the toy store, then you should practice saying no to them. Aside from that, you should also learn to say no to your friends, if they want you to out with them for drinks. Saying no would not just feel liberating, but it can also help you save some dough.

* Shopping items on sale. If you just happen to be in a store because you have free time, and you found items that are on sale, then you might be tempted in acquiring them immediately.

However, before you make a drastic move, try to think about whether you really need the item or not. Although the item may cost only half of its original price, you still should not buy it if you don't really need it.

* Making a list for the grocery. When you are shopping at a grocery store, chances are you would end up going over your budget if you won't bring a list with you. Thus, it is a good idea to make a list of all the things that you really need. Aside from that though, make sure to take note of the prices of the grocery items, so that you already have an idea how much you are going to spend when you buy your groceries.

9. Shop online. Shopping online can give you an opportunity to save some amounts of cash. If you do your research, you would find out that most items found through the internet are more affordable than those that are sold in local stores. The reason behind this is that, online stores have lesser overhead expenses. Thus, shopping the modern way should help you save up some cash.

* Take advantage of online auction sites. When you take a look around your own house, you may realize that you have lots of used things, which you are not using anymore. If these items are still in good condition, then you should sell them in online auctions sites. Earning more money is also a good way to saving more. Aside from that, while you are earning online, you can actually get rid of the clutter and have more space in your house.

10. Take advantage of your credit card without getting buried into debt.

* Credit card promotions are offered every now and then, in which it can provide you a way to save some money through gift cards,

gift checks, or discounts on certain stores and restaurants. Some can even offer a cash back option, for a certain amount of credits used, or when you purchase from certain stores.

* Avoid spending through credit cards. Spending through credit cards is one of the best ways to pile up your debt. Thus, if you want to save more money, you should purchase on cash basis only. Save the credit cards for emergency situations only. Every item you purchase with the use of your credit card can add more to your existing debt and your monthly surcharge; thus, it is time that you leave them at home when you go out to shop.

* The card's annual fee. There are credit cards today that offer free annual fees, while some do not. Credit card companies that charge annual fees may have added features into their cards. However, in most cases, such features are not very applicable to lots of people. Thus, it is best to choose cards that won't charge you annual fees, so that you can save more money on a yearly basis.

* Rate reductions. If you are carrying a balance in your card and it has been like that for quite some time, then try to negotiate for rate reductions. There is a good chance that your credit card company would agree to this. This is because they don't want to risk more defaults, since it is bad for their business. They would rather ask lesser amounts of money from you, than suffer the consequences of more defaults

* Take care of your credit card debt. One of the things that can add more to your monthly expenses is your credit card debt. This is because the higher your debt becomes, the more you need to pay in terms of its interest. In other words, you may end up paying for the interest each month, without even touching the principal amount you owe. Clear your credit card debt by applying for a low cost loan, so that you can breathe easier.

* Check out your credit card points. Lots of credit card companies today offer rewards in relation to the points that you have collected whenever you use your card. If you have gathered enough points, you should check out the available items that you can redeem it for. Aside from items though, some companies may also agree to waive some fees associated with your account in exchange for the points.

11. Be your own DIY guy/girl. Before tossing out an item, you should see if you can repair it yourself first. By doing that, you would be able to save money by not having to purchase a new one. To fix something up, you can always ask your friends for tips regarding it. Aside from that, you can also check out some troubleshooting tips through the internet.

12. Gaming at nights. If you and your friends are quite fond of going out at nights, especially on weekends, then you should invite them for a gaming night at your place. This would help you all in saving lots of money. All you have to do is to take out your favorite board game, buy some snacks and drinks, and enjoy a good time at your place, without spending lots of money in bars or coffee shops.

13. Watching movies at your place. If your family wants to spend some time with you by watching a movie in town, you should consider watching one at your own house. Renting a video at a shop near your place should do the trick. Pair it up with some popcorn and sodas and your family would have a great time with you, while you are not worrying about the total cost.

14. Swaps are good. Swapping your unused things for new ones is yet another means of saving money. Swapping can be done through the internet, with your friends, or with certain shops. You can swap your shoes, books, music, movies, games, gadgets, and

more, for items that you want to have so that you won't have to spend a dime in getting it.

15. Buying magazines at a newsstand. If you are quite fond of certain types of magazines, buying them at the newsstand should be avoided. This is because they are usually priced too high when you purchase them from these types of stores. To save money, you can always subscribe directly to the magazine. Aside from that, check out their websites, since they might even offer e-magazines, which you can conveniently download into your computer for free or for a very affordable price.

16. The lottery. If you are fond of playing the lottery, you should seriously think about your odds of winning it. There is very less likelihood that you would hit the jackpot in the lottery, and each time you play it, you are actually spending more cash. Thus, if you simply want to be entertained, then you should consider playing at a casino, since the cost is pretty much the same, the odds would be better, and it can provide you with more entertainment.

17. Travel the world without spending a fortune.

* In traveling, one of the best things that you can do in order to save huge amounts of money is to book way ahead of time. This is true, especially if you book online. Lots of airlines are actually offering discounts for early bookings today. Aside from that, you should also keep in mind that booking a vacation package is also more affordable, than booking your hotel, flights, and cars separately.

* Your travel times. To save up some money, you should be flexible when it comes to your traveling times. For example, in booking flights, if you are not in a hurry, red-eye flights are actually good to book in terms of saving cash, although you may not want your

children traveling late. Aside from such types of flights, traveling to certain vacation spots during off-season can also be a good idea, when it comes to saving on costs.

* Talking to a travel agent. If you are not getting anywhere in trying to book more affordable fights and accommodations online, you should know that many travel websites have travel agents working for them. They are usually reachable through their 800 numbers on a 24 hour basis. Thus, giving them a call should provide you with the assistance that you need, in order to find the package that you really want.

* Having an affordable vacation. During the holidays, people usually go to distant places to spend their vacations on. However, if your finances are quite tight or you simply want to save money, then you should consider having a vacation at the city where you are living it. By doing that, you would be able to rediscover your place. Aside from that, since you won't be going out of the place, you won't have to spend quite a hefty sum of money for your flights.

* Prior to getting travel insurance, you should decide to go on a trip first. Thus, if you have previously acquired an annual insurance, then you should not renew it, unless you are going to travel soon.

18. Going from one building to another. If you are at a city center, where you anticipate moving from one building to another to look for certain types of items, then you should park your car at a garage or parking area, which is located centrally. This way, it would allow you to leave it there, instead of driving it around town and consume more gasoline. With that, you would be saving more money, and even get some exercise.

19. Car rental insurance. If a car rental company offers you their own car rental insurance, you should stop for a moment, and think about your own auto insurance. Most auto insurance companies today provide policies, where your auto insurance coverage would also apply to your rental car. Thus, if this is the case, then you should decline the offer. However, it is still best to call your insurance provider for that, just to make sure.

20. Riding a bike. When you are on your way to a place where it is a bit far for a walk, then you should make use of your bike. Biking can prevent you from using more fossil fuel, which can harm the planet, aside from costing you money. With that, you should always ride your bike, so that you consume lesser amounts of fuel, and save more money.

21. It is always best to use your bank's ATM machine, whether you want to process a withdrawal, fund transfer, or even just checking for your balance. This is because when you do these things in another bank's ATM machine, you would be charged by that bank, as well as your own bank for certain fees. 22. Bundle your insurance policies. There are certain insurance providers today, which can offer not just auto insurance policies, but also homeowners, and other forms of insurances. If you want to save some money, you should ask your provider for possible discounts if you bundle your policies. When you do that, aside from saving money, it would also become more convenient for you, since you won't have to deal with paying different providers.

* If you want to reduce your monthly insurance premiums, then you should recheck your insurance coverage for possible deductibles. Deductibles are the amount of money that you need to shoulder in an event of an accident. Your premium would decrease when you have it, since part of the risk would be transferred to you from the company.

* When you pay your insurance premiums, you should do it way ahead of time. This is because insurance companies can offer you with more discounts when you pay it before the due date. Thus, it is best if you ask your insurance provider about this, so that you would be able to take advantage of it. 40. Have a savings account in more friendly banks. There are certain banks these days that can charge you so many fees that you won't even get the chance to earn any kind of interest. One of the fees that are quite common for some banks is called the maintenance fees. Thus, if you read your bank's booklet and found this term, then you should consider switching banks as soon as possible.

* Get more quotes. When it is the time of the year to renew your auto insurance, you should not hesitate in shopping around for the most affordable rates. A good way of doing this is to get free quotes from different insurance providers. Before you decide to switch to another insurer though, make sure to consider the coverage they can provide, to be on the safe side.

* Opting for a more basic insurance coverage. To save up some money in terms of your insurance premiums, you can always tell your insurance provider to drop your collision and comprehensive coverage. This is a wise move, especially if your car is quite old. However, you need to be aware that dropping the said items from your declarations page would mean that you would be responsible for the cost of repairs to your own vehicle, whenever you are involved with an accident, in which you are the at-fault party.

23. Cutting your home phone bills. Landlines or home phone services usually cost more than their VOIP counterparts. Thus, you should consider switching to a VOIP phone service and just maintain your mobile phones. Aside from that, you should also check with your local phone service provider, if they can provide you with the most basic service to cut down on costs.

24. Go to the grocery store after eating and not before. When you go to a store to shop for groceries, it is always best to do it after grabbing a snack, or eating lunch. This is because shopping in groceries when you are hungry can make you purchase food items, which you really do not need. In most cases, when you get home from shopping and eat lunch, you would realize later on that you have gone over your budget, for taking in too many food items.

25. Shopping for clothes. In buying your own clothing, you may have a tendency to purchase those that are heavily advertised by celebrities. Designer label clothes are very expensive. Although they are good in terms of quality and design, you can actually find lots of products today, which are equally good but are more affordable. Thus, avoid such types of clothing, so that you can save some money.

26. Keeping up with appearances. If you have a tendency to buy something that you saw your friend or neighbor has recently bought, then you should cut that costly habit. This is because you may end up buying lots of things you don't need. Aside from that, you don't even know how your neighbor got it; and, they might even have used their credit cards for it.

27. Buying a car wisely. Whenever you want to buy a brand new car, a couple of factors you want to consider would be the car's fuel efficiency and reliability. When you focus on these factors, it can actually save you lots of money in the long run. Thus, you should do your research about the cars you are considering purchasing soon, so that you can have the one that can help you save more money. 93. How to prevent shopping by impulse. Making impulse buys, especially if you use your credit card for it can pile up your debts. To ensure that this is not the case, whenever you have the urge to purchase something, you should spend around a minute or two in thinking about whether you really

need it or not. If not, then you simply have to let go of the urge, and save your hard earned cash.

* Trading your car. Having a new used vehicle is not such a bad idea, especially if you want to save some cash. You should also consider this, if the car that you currently have piles up your expenses by consuming more gas, and offering little space for your family. There are lots of car supermarkets these days, which can offer you a quality used vehicle that has a price that is just a fraction of the brand new one. Check them out, so that you can save more cash.

28. Your gym membership. In order to have a healthier body, you may be visiting the gym on a regular basis. However, if your busy schedule prevents you from visiting it at least thrice a week, then you should cancel it. With your hectic schedule, you should workout at your own place from now on. Aside from saving more time, you can also save some money since you won't have to deal with membership fees.

29. Cut down your drinking habit. Aside from the fact that drinking can cause negative effects to your health, it actually adds up on your monthly cost of living. If you are used to drinking a bottle or two of your favorite beer each night, you should cut it down to just a couple of beers only on weekends. By doing that, you are doing your body a favor, as well as your pocket. 55. Quit smoking. Smoking is one of the leading causes of certain types of diseases all around the world. Aside from that, cigarettes also continue to become more and more expensive these days. Thus, you should find ways to quit it. When you quit smoking, you can lessen your risks to certain diseases, smell good, and save some money along the way.

30. Use the internet. If you are in need of a new recipe, a new guide to playing the guitar, or a new manual for self-development, you no longer have to go to the bookstore and spend lots of cash for it. What you can do is to access websites for the information that you need. Aside from offering you informative articles about the topic you are interested in, you can also find lots of eBooks on the web that are for free.

31. Extended warranties. Extended warranties are usually available for popular electronic devices. They are usually offered so that you would have a warranty that extends for more than just a year. Before you take advantage of it though, you should stop and think if you really need it. In most cases, a warranty for six to twelve months is already enough. Just make sure to choose an electronic device that is made in good quality, so that you won't have to worry about extended warranties.

32. Avoid the vending machine. When you want a snack and you visit the vending machine for it, most likely, you would be paying a lot more for the foods that you eat, than if you were buying them from the grocery store. Therefore, the next time you purchase goods from the grocery, make sure to include your snack food items. By doing that, you can simply bring them with you, each time you report for work.

33. Buying medicines. In buying medicines, the factors that can affect their prices are their brands. Thus, if you want to save money, then you should stick to generic brands. These generic medicines are actually equally effective as its high end counterparts. Just take note of the name of the medicine prescribed by your doctor and not the brand, so that you can save some cash. 34. Visiting the coffee shop. If you simply love coffee and you often find yourself going to coffee shops for it, then you should learn how to brew your own coffee soon. There are lots of

coffee-making products available in the market today, which can allow you to make cups of delicious coffee in just a matter of minutes. Purchase one soon and you would be able to enjoy your favorite cup of coffee, without having to go out of your place and spending more money.

35. Go with water. When you are thirsty, whether you are at a movie theater or at the mall, you should skip soda, beer, or juice, and stick to water. This is because water is more affordable than the other drinking beverages, and in some places, it can even be offered for free. Aside from saving more money by drinking water, it can also help you stay fit, since it is not loaded with calories.

36. Collect reusable bags. When you have a bunch of reusable bags at your place, then you can bring it with you when you buy your groceries. There are certain grocery stores these days, which can offer you discounts, tokens, or coupons, if you are going to bring your own bag for your purchased goods. By doing that, you won't just be saving money, but you could also be saving the world by using lesser plastic bags

37. Driving at nights. Whenever you are driving at nights, you can actually save up some money by opening your car windows. By doing that, you would not have to turn on your air conditioner, and save up some gas in the process. With lesser gasoline consumed on a regular basis, you would be able to save more money.

38. Make sure your tires are properly inflated. Making sure that your tires are properly inflated can prolong its life and save you some money in the process. Aside from that, it can also ensure that handling your car would be easy. Moreover, when the tires are properly inflated, you can also be assured that your car's fuel efficiency is at its maximum levels.

Feed Your Piggy Bank!

* Get your car checked regularly. Having your car go through routine maintenance actually offers a lot of benefits to you. Aside from making sure that your car is in top condition, it could also prevent damages, which can cost you a lot of money. Just make sure to find a reliable mechanic, so that he won't always tell you to replace something, just to make a quick buck.

* Your car's air filter. Cleaning your car's air filter will take you a long way when it comes to saving money. This is because a clean air filter can improve your vehicle's fuel efficiency. With that, you can be assured that your gasoline consumption would be maintained at reasonable levels. Just check out your car's manual in doing it, so that you can clean the air filter soon.

39. Free parking. When you go around town, you may find that lots of places require payment for parking, especially those that are near certain landmarks. However, if you are patient enough, you should be able to find a place that offers free parking. You may have to walk a few blocks towards your destination for it, but it would be worth it, especially if you practice this regularly.

40. Choosing services you really need. Each year, you should evaluate what services you really need and what services you don't need. You should ask yourself whether you really need to have cable television, landline, magazine subscriptions, and such. Try to check which services you really need to have a decent way of living, and stick only with them. Drop the other ones you don't need, so that you can save money.

41. Play online games. If you have an internet connection at your place, it is far better to play online games, instead of purchasing more video games for your gaming console. There are lots of online gaming sites today, which can offer you the kind of entertainment that you want for free. With that, you won't have to pay for video

games that are pretty expensive, which can help you save more money.

42. Don't use your dryer. In washing your clothes, you may have gotten used to utilizing the dryer of your washing machine to dry your clothes up. However, if you want to save money, then you should line-dry your clothes instead. This simply means getting yourself a clothesline or a rack where you can dry your clothes on. By doing that, you are lengthening the lifespan of your machine, aside from minimizing energy consumption.

43. Focus on your collection. Lots of people like to have a collection of certain things, which they consider as a hobby. Some people like to collect caps, while others enjoy collecting bags. If you are one of them, then you should think whether the things you are collecting can really provide you with what you need. If not, then you should try to stop your costly habit. Instead, you should try to sell your collection, so that you can add more money to your savings account.

44. Customer rewards programs. There are grocery stores and even bookstores today, which offer customer rewards programs. If the store that you usually purchase items from offers it, then you should sign up with them. Although it takes some time to rack up some points, it can still provide you with something to extend your budget. Aside from that, some of these reward programs can also give you coupons and discounts on certain items.

45. Personalize your gifts. Whenever you hand out gifts for birthdays, Christmas, and such, it is always best to personalize them, in order to increase its value. Aside from making the present more meaningful though, personalizing gifts can also offer you a way to save up some cash. Thus, make use of your imagination, so

that you can save up some money, while making your friends happy.

46. Finding relief from stress. If you need to relieve yourself from stress, there is no need to spend lots of money for it. As long as you know some meditation techniques or yoga, then you wouldn't have to go to spas or massage parlors to relax. Aside from that, you can even just sit or lie down and listen to soothing music in order to get over a stressful day at work.

47. Wash your hands properly. Cleaning your hands thoroughly after going to the comfort room, or touching different types of things like money, books, among others, is one of the best ways to prevent diseases to affect you. Keeping yourself from viruses and bacteria can help in saving money, since you won't have to deal with medical bills and medicine costs.

48. Gain the support of your family. If you want to save more money, you should tell your family all about it. When you do that, you can actually gain their support. If your whole family supports you, you can all work out together in order to minimize your costs. They can all help in minimizing energy and water consumption. Aside from that, they could also understand better if you won't be eating out as often as you usually do.

49 Take up gardening. Gardening can be fun, aside from the fact that it can help you save more money. When you already have a garden, you won't have to spend extra cash for cabbages, tomatoes, oranges, and other fruits and vegetables, since you can conveniently grow them yourself. By doing that, on top of saving money, you can also ensure that you are consuming organic food items.

50. Check your mobile phone bill thoroughly. To save more money, one of the best ways to do it is to check your phone bill for the services that you have enrolled it with. Try to carefully evaluate these services, so that you can properly decide whether you really need them or not. To get rid of some, all you need to do is to contact your service provider and tell them about it.

51. Make your own wine. If you love to drink wines so much, then you may have already spent lots of money in purchasing bottles of your favorite drinks. There are actually affordable wine making kits available in the market today, and they usually come with everything, which include the ingredients. By using such kits, you no longer have to purchase expensive wines, since you can already make them yourself.

Chapter 5- Does Money Grow in Groups?

Depending on how exposed one is to this style of financial discussions, the money growing in groups concept, can be considered fairly new and really undiscovered territory. The following points are laid out in the hope that some clearer understanding can be gotten from this type of concept.

Depending on how exposed one is to this style of financial discussions, the money growing in groups concept, can be considered fairly new and really undiscovered territory. The following points are laid out in the hope that some clearer understanding can be gotten from this type of concept.

For some participants this would just be a safe environment to bounce ideas about and get feedback on proposals and business formulas, while for others it may be an opportunity to present a business plan to encourage other to participate with the intention of acquiring some form of group financing and commitment.

However this may not be well received if the participants are not inclined to attend, for business sourcing reasons.

To be able to grow one's individual resources faster when pooled as a group can be rather effective. When the combined resources are much bigger and more impactful the advantages it presents due to the availability of such funds will definitely bring about more opportunities, than when compared to the singular funds of the individual.

This style also presents other advantages such as being able to brainstorm and discuss in depth the impact and repercussion a particular business endeavor may bring about.

As a group more views can be expressed and more often than not surprising discoveries are made. These surprising discoveries can actually help to keep those planning the business out of trouble which would otherwise not be foreseen.

Small Step for You, Giant Leap for Your Financial Success

Most people think that things done in a big way is the only way to gain success that can be felt and enjoyed. This is far from true especially when the big efforts don't yield the desired positive outcomes expected within the time frame projected.

Mentally and physically, taking small steps would definitely yield better result in many ways, some of which are listed below:

When things are done in a big way, expectations are also high and everything connected to the huge commitment is also expected to be big in its returns.

Feed Your Piggy Bank!

This can have a detrimental effect on the mindset of all concerned and connected to the endeavor. When things start going wrong, and the projected outcomes are not visible or even worse not possible, the feeling of dejection sets in and this negativity can contribute to the individual losing focus and giving up altogether.

Learning to make small adjustments, especially when it comes to starting a saving plan will be a better option, as this small start will not overwhelm the individual and cause the exercise to be abandoned at the first sign of a challenge.

Another advantage of starting small is that the actual exercise of saving will help to give the individual more confidence once the results of such savings becomes evident.

With the ability to create this amount of savings clearly possible the individual may then decide to venture into taking on a slightly bigger savings challenge. Continue to challenge yourself until such time that a substantial healthy savings plan becomes a normal part of your budgeting exercise.

CHAPTER 6- SHOULD YOU RELY ON PENSIONS WITHOUT SAVINGS?

There are some very obvious differences between the saving and pension platforms and it would actually be up to the individual to decide on which is best suited to them.

Elements such as character traits of the individual and his or her earning capacity would have to be taken into consideration when making the choice between the two options.

There is also the need to ensure the earning capability of the individual is both consistent and guarded. Other deciding contributing factor may include the current lifestyle and future lifestyle the individual expects to enjoy.

Being able to factor in as many points that will play a dominant role in making an informed choice is very important indeed. Therefore there is a need to be a discerning as possible to ensure the choice made now will bring forth the desired results in the future.

Perhaps the most telling difference between the two options is the fact that savings plans are mostly designed in a way where access to the cash is almost always easy and instantaneous.

However the same cannot be said for that on the pension plan where there is virtually no access to the funds until a certain age is reached.

For those who don't consider themselves disciplined enough to keep from withdrawing from a savings plan, the pension is a better option.

For those who have a knack for making successful investments, opting for the pension plan not only be rather restrictive, but will also be of no present value to them.

From the taxation angle there are also some differences to be enjoyed which vary between the two categories. There is some tax relief that can be enjoyed for contributions to the pension fund which is not applicable to that of a saving plan.

However the saving interests are not taxable whereas the pension income does have some percentage of tax tagged to it.

ABOUT THE AUTHOR

Deborah is a certified thrift manager. She would spend her time couponing to save on shopping and would even wake up in the middle of the night to move her lawn, when electricity is cheaper.

Because of her resourcefulness and determination to save, Deborah has successfully set aside enough money to send all her children to college.